I'D RATHER BE 40 THAN PREGNANT

By Karen Kavet
with help from Linda Gordon, Karen Gershman
and Kathy Lamay
Designed and Illustrated by Martin Riskin

Copyright © 1983

By IVORY TOWER PUBLISHING COMPANY, INC.

Published simultaneously in Canada by
Encore Sales Inc. of Downsview, Ontario.

Manufactured in the United States of America.

First Printing, May 1983

IVORY TOWER PUBLISHING COMPANY, INC.
125 Walnut Street, Watertown, Massachusetts 02172
TEL: (617) 923-1111   TELEX: 955-439 Intel. Div. - ITOP

P9-ARL-263

INTRODUCTION

Some women are terrified at the thought of being 40. Our society is very youth-oriented with tremendous emphasis placed on firm bodies and smooth faces. How quick we are to forget all the problems that go with youth and inexperience. *I'd Rather Be 40 Than Pregnant* will put some perspective back into your life and probably convince you that your present age is a pretty terrific one.

I'd rather be 40 than...

Waking up for 2 a.m. feedings, changing diapers and emptying them in that cold toilet.

I'd rather be 40 than...

Living at home and having everyone tell me
what to do, and bickering with siblings over
cars, clothes, and chores.

I'd rather be 40 than...

Too scared to enjoy sex and too concerned
over what men are saying about me.

I'd rather be 40 than...

Have to leave parties early because the babysitter
has an 11 o'clock curfew.

I'd rather be 40 than...

In an entry level position again, earning $86.43 each week after taxes, and being asked at every interview if I have EXPERIENCE.
Let me tell you - I HAVE EXPERIENCE.

I'd rather be 40 than...

An awkward teenager having to struggle with
inept 17-year-old lovers in the back seat of cars.

I'd rather be 40 than...

Be unable to feel secure when ordering wine
at a restaurant.

I'd rather be 40 than...

Have repair men treat me like a complete idiot.
Come to think of it, these chauvinists treat
all women that way.

I'd rather be 40 than...

Dressing kids for cold weather and then undressing them again when they have to go to the bathroom.

I'd rather be 40 than...

Have boys dunk me at the beach.

I'd rather be 40 than...

Not have any investments.

I'd rather be 40 than...

Worry about virginity or worry about reaching orgasm.

I'd rather be 40 than...

Dependent again on in-laws, babysitters, and
play groups for my freedom.

I'd rather be 40 than...

Waiting longingly for "Sesame Street" to begin
each day.

I'd rather be 40 than...

Wonder why I got the job.

I'd rather be 40 than...

Worry about sitting home, even once,
on a Saturday night.

I'd rather be 40 than...

Have no one respect my opinion.

I'd rather be 40 than...

Be unable to afford to even walk through the
designer sections of department stores.

I'd rather be 40 than...

Be flustered and unable to handle a risque
conversation with an exciting man,
or be unable to understand a dirty joke.

I'd rather be 40 and...

picked up elegantly for a date rather than
meet men at dating bars.

I'd rather be 40 than...

Lacking the brains, gumption, and confidence to direct my life in the ways that make me happiest.

I'd rather be 40 than...

Believe all the things men whisper in your ear
when they are trying to get you into bed.

I'd rather be 40 than...

Foolish enough to sit home waiting for his phone call.

I'd rather be 40 than...

Worry about "breaking out" if I eat a hot fudge sundae.

I'd rather be 40 than...

Not have any real gold jewelry.

I'd rather be 40 than...

Too immature to recognize what colors and clothes are right for me, or be unable to use makeup properly.

I'd rather be 40 than...

Be unable to express myself because of demands
of children, husband, or low level bosses.

I'd rather be 40 and...

able to spend weekends shopping or visiting museums rather than sitting through Bambi and Snow White matinee reruns with the kids.

I'd rather be 40 than...

Have to rely on TV soaps as my sole source of
adventure. It's nice to have a few experiences
of your own to rival those stories.

I'd rather be 40 than...

Dress and primp all day for some immature goon
who couldn't possibly appreciate beauty or charm.

I'd rather be 40 than...

Never to have traveled to exotic places, and be
unable to vacation in warm climates.

I'd rather be 40 than...

Be unable to order a drink or cash a check.

I'd rather be 40 than...

Be flustered when it comes time to leave a tip.

I'd rather be 40 than...

Worry about the kids on their first night
away from home.

I'd rather be 40 than...

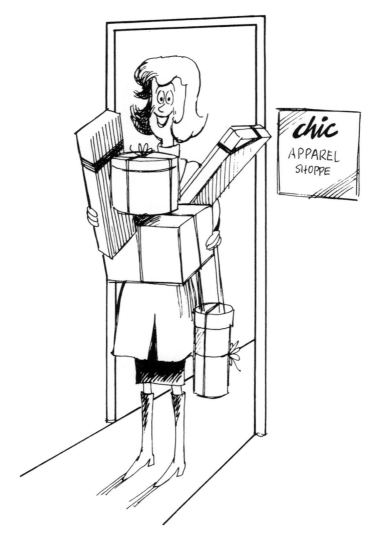

Worry about every penny in my budget and never have
enough money for an occasional splurge,
or even to afford really sheer stockings.

I'd rather be 40 than...

Have to deal with roommates and family and other
encroachers on my privacy.

I'd rather be 40 than...

Be unable to attract and carry on a conversation
with intelligent men.

I'd rather be 40 than...

Worry about exams or getting into graduate school
or finding a first job.

I'd rather be 40 than...

Travel with young children.

I'd rather be 40 than...

Be unable to smoothly put down propositions
from a drunk chauvinist.

I'd rather be 40 than...

Not have the time to play tennis or go to
dance classes each week.

I'd rather be 40 than...

Refused credit and charge cards at department stores
and not have any in my own name.

I'd rather be 40 than...

Get no respect at a ritzy store.

I'd rather be 40 and...

able to smoke and express myself freely
in front of my parents.

I'd rather be 40 than...

Unable to handle an obscene phone call.

I'd rather be 40 than...

Not know how to eat an artichoke.

I'd rather be 40 than...

Picked up for a date on a motorcycle.

I'd rather be 40 than...

Not have my own opinions about art.

I'd rather be 40 than...

Supporting pediatricians and orthodontists.

I'd rather be 40 than...

Worry about a "burp" ending up all over my shoulder.

I'd rather be 40 than...

Have my husband's salary match his neck size
rather than his waist size.

I'd rather be 40 than...

Have to take out loans for kids rather than vacations.

I'd rather be 40 than...

Feel like I have to keep up with every fashion style.

I'd rather be 40 than...

Have older, sophisticated men tell me I'm too young.

I'd rather be 40 than...

Get embarrassed at an adult movie.

I'd rather be 40 than...

Wonder if there will be any money left in the
Social Security fund by the time I reach 65.

I'd rather be 40 and...

be settled in my own home surrounded
by things I love.

I'd rather be 40 than...

Have to train the puppy again; now he even
walks himself.

I'd rather be 40 than...

Think it is important to run around every night
just to keep myself busy.

I'd rather be 40 and...

know just what it takes to make "him" feel good.

I'd rather be 40 and...

able to know when using four letter words
is appropriate.

I'd rather be 40 than...

Worry about an invitation to the Prom.

I'd rather be 40 and...

have a few super recipes really down pat.

I'd rather be 40 than...

Subjected to the punk rock and new wave music
that kids think is "in" today; the music of my day
had lyrics you could understand.

I'd rather be 40 than...

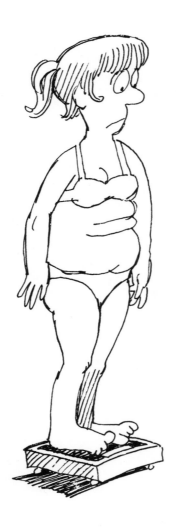

Still waiting for the "baby fat" to disappear.

I'd rather be 40 and...

able to afford a housekeeper; better, to be mature
enough to realize that the house doesn't have
to be immaculate.

I'd rather be 40 and...

know the value of a good friend.

I'd rather be 40 and...

never have to take public transportation.

I'd rather be 40 and...

have my mother ask for my opinion.

I'd rather be 40 than...

Be frantic when my husband travels
and I have to get kids to school by 7:30 a.m. -
at opposite ends of town.

I'd rather be 40 and...

have a weekend "get away" at the beach or mountains.

I'd rather be 40 and...

have the kids old enough to help.

I'd rather be 40 and...

collect real art rather than posters.

I'd rather be 40 and...

have elegant dinners for twelve rather than
BYOB parties for fifty.

I'd rather be 40 than...

Unable to say NO to a door-to-door salesman.

I'd rather be 40 and...

hear my kids say "You know, Mom, you were right."

I'd rather be 40 and...

able to finally throw out all the back issues of
"Parent" magazine, along with Dr. Spock.

I'd rather be 40 and...

have spent so many years with the man I married
that I know all his faults, and still love him -
perhaps even more.

I'd rather be 40 and...

have a favorite vacation spot where everyone
knows my name.

I'd rather be 40 than...

Have to go on a panic diet each spring
to fit into a bikini.

I'd rather be 40 and...

have a fine grasp of all the latest financial jargon.

I'd rather be 40 and...

able to enjoy watching my children mature into
intelligent adults.

I'd rather be 40 and...

appreciate the freedom of control top pantyhose
rather than girdles and garter belts.

I'd rather be 40 and...

really believe that I'm not getting older,
I'm getting better.

I'd rather be 40 than...

Using bricks, bean bags, and blow-ups for furniture.

I'd rather be 40 than...

Have waiters ask for my ID when ordering a drink.

I'd rather be 40 than...

Unable to change a tire or know how to start my car
on really cold days.

I'd rather be 40 and...

understand the importance of keeping fit
to maintain my figure.

I'd rather be 40 than...

Kissing all those frogs while looking for my
handsome prince.

I'd rather be 40 than...

Constantly embarrassed by my kids in public places.

I'd rather be 40 than...

Unable to gauge the amount of alcohol I can tolerate.

I'd rather be 40 than...

Always talked into activities I can't handle,
in weather I don't like.